# *Sufism* & GOOD CHARACTER

*In the name of Allāh, Most Gracious Most Merciful.*

*All praise be to Allāh, Lord of the Worlds, and peace and blessings be upon His Messenger Muḥammad, Mercy to the Worlds.*

# Sufism & Good Character

*Prophetic Guidance on the Spiritual Path*

Imām Ẓafar Aḥmad ʿUthmānī

being the final chapter of his monumental *Iʿlāʾ al-Sunan*
with commentary from ʿAlī al-Qārī and Kumushkhānawī

*Translated by*
Faraz Fareed Rabbani

White Thread
PRESS

First Edition November 2004
Reprint October 2012, May 2020



ISBN 978-0-9728358-3-1

*Published by*
White Thread Press
WT Press Limited
London • UK
www.whitethreadpress.com
info@whitethreadpress.com

Distributed in the UK by
Azhar Academy Ltd. London
sales@azharacademy.com
Tel: +44 (208) 911 9797

Library of Congress Cataloging-in-Publication Data

ʿUthmānī, Ẓafar Aḥmad, 1892–1974.
[*Iʿlā' al-Sunan*. English]
Sufism & Good Character: Prophetic Guidance on the Spiritual Path / by Ẓafar Aḥmad ʿUthmānī; translated by Faraz Fareed Rabbani.— 1st ed.
p. cm.
"Being the final chapter of his monumental *Iʿlā' al-Sunan* with commentary from Al-Qārī and Al-Kumushkhānawī."
ISBN 0-9728358-3-0 (pbk. : alk. paper)
1. Islam—Customs and practices. 2. Islam—Rituals. 3. Sufism. 4. Muslims—Conduct of life. I. Title: Sufism and Good Character. II. Qārī, ʿAlī. III. Ahmed Ziyāüddīn Gümüshanevī, ca. 1813-1894. IV. Title.
BP174.U8613 2004
297.4–dc22

2004017409

♾ Printed and bound in Turkey on premium acid-free paper. The paper used in this book meets the minimum requirement of ANSI/NISO Z39.48-1992 (R 1997) (Permanence of Paper). The binding material has been chosen for strength and durability.

Cover design by Farooq Ahmed and ARM
Book design and typography by ARM

*As for those who strive for Us, We surely guide them to Our paths, and indeed Allāh is with those of excellence*

The Qur'ān 29:69

# TRANSLITERATION KEY

ء (أ إ) ’ (A slight catch in the breath. It is also used to indicate where the *hamza* has been dropped from the beginning of a word.)

ا a, ā

ب b

ت t

ث th (Should be pronounced as the *th* in *thin* or *thirst*.)

ج j

ح ḥ (Tensely breathed *h* sound.)

خ kh (Pronounced like the *ch* in Scottish *loch* with the mouth hollowed to produce a full sound.)

د d

ذ dh (Should be pronounced as the *th* in *this* or *that*.)

ر r

ز z

س s

ش sh

ص ṣ (A heavy *s* pronounced far back in the mouth with the mouth hollowed to produce a full sound.)

ض ḍ (A heavy *d/dh* pronounced far back in the mouth with the mouth hollowed to produce a full sound.)

ط ṭ (A heavy *t* pronounced far back in the mouth with the mouth hollowed to produce a full sound.)

ظ ẓ (A heavy *dh* pronounced far back in the mouth with the mouth hollowed to produce a full sound.)

ع ʿ, ʿa, ʿi, ʿu (Pronounced from the throat.)

غ gh (Pronounced like a throaty French *r* with the mouth hollowed to produce a full sound.)

ف f

ق q (A guttural *q* sound with the mouth hollowed to produce a full sound.)

ك k

ل l

م m

ن n

و w, ū, u.

ه h

ي y, ī, i

ﷺ *Ṣalla ’Llāhu ʿalayhi wa sallam*—used following the mention of the Messenger Muḥammad, translated as, “May Allāh bless him and give him peace.”

عليه السلام *ʿAlayhi ’l-sallam*—used following the mention of a prophet or messenger of Allāh, translated as, “May the peace of Allāh be upon him.”

رضي الله عنه *Raḍiya ’Llāhu ʿanhu*—used following the mention of a Companion of the Messenger ﷺ, translated as, “May Allāh be pleased with him.”

رضي الله عنهم *Raḍiya ’Llāhu ʿanhum*—used following the mention of more than one Companion of the Messenger (and also after a female Companion in this work for lack of an appropriate glyph), translated as, “May Allāh be pleased with them.”

# Contents

# Translator's Preface

This book is a clear presentation of the importance of Sufism in Islam and its role in developing good character—of which the Prophet ﷺ said, "On the Day of Resurrection, nothing will weigh heavier upon the scales than good character" (*Abū Dāwūd* and *Tirmidhī*). At the heart of the book are 80 ḥadīths of the Prophet Muḥammad ﷺ that relate to the spiritual way. The author, Imām Ẓafar ʿUthmānī, explains the practices of Sufism through these noble ḥadīths.

To further the benefit of the book, commentary on many of the ḥadīths has been added from the classic works of two great jurists and ḥadīth masters, Mullā ʿAlī al-Qārī and Mawlānā Aḥmad Ḍiyā' al-Dīn al-Kumushkhānawī. Notes explaining key terms and concepts have also been included where necessary.

**What is Sufism?**

The great North African Sufi, Shaykh Aḥmad Zarrūq, gave perhaps the clearest and most complete definition of Sufism. He said it is "sincerity in turning to Allāh," and explained that "the necessary condition of sincerity of approach is that it be what the Truth Most High accepts, and by the means He accepts. Now, something lacking its necessary condition cannot exist: "And He does not accept unbelief for His servants" (Qur'ān 39:7), so one must realize true faith (*īmān*), "and if you show gratitude, He will accept it of you" (Qur'ān 39:7), which entails applying Islam. So, there is no Sufism without comprehension of Sacred Law, as the outward rules of Allāh Most High are not known save through it. And there is no comprehension of Sacred Law without Sufism, as works are nothing without sincerity of approach, as expressed by the words of Imām Mālik (may Allāh have mercy on him):

> He who practices Sufism without learning Sacred Law corrupts his faith, while he who learns Sacred Law without practicing Sufism corrupts himself. Only he who combines the two proves true (*Īqāẓ al-Himam fī Sharḥ al-Ḥikam*, 5-6; from *The Reliance of the Traveler*, w9.3, 862).

Similarly, Shaykh Muṣṭafā Najā explained that the basis of the spiritual way is "absolute uprightness (*al-istiqāma al-tāmma*), being with Allāh, having presence of heart in one's slavehood, and conforming to the Qur'ān and Sunna in every breath, step, spiritual experience, and state. Its pillar is keeping the company of the people of divine knowledge and Sacred Law, and making much remembrance with presence of heart" (*Kitāb Kashf al-Asrār li Tanwīr al-Afkār* 41).

This is the understanding of Imām Ẓafar, who combined between profound knowledge of the Sacred Law, and steadfast commitment to the path of Sufism and its principles.

### Imām Ẓafar Aḥmad ᶜUthmānī (1310–1394 AH)

He was the authoritative scholar of the Islamic sciences, the Qur'ānic exegete, ḥadīth expert, jurist, and Sufi, Ẓafar Aḥmad ibn Laṭīf ᶜUthmānī al-Thānawī.[1] He was born the 13th of Rabīᶜ al-Awwal, 1310 AH. His mother died when he was only three, so his grandmother raised him. She was a righteous woman who had performed the *ḥajj*.[2] She raised him well, and he benefited from her rectitude and piety (*taqwā*).

1 This biography is adapted from Shaykh ᶜAbd al-Fattāḥ ᶜAbū-Ghudda's preface to *Iᶜlā' al-Sunan* (p. 8–10), which contains a 553 page introduction to the ḥadīth sciences. The preface has also been published separately as *Qawā'id fī ᶜUlūm al-Ḥadīth* (Principles of the Science of Ḥadīth). The biography has been abbreviated for reasons of clarity and space.

2 In the days before commercial aviation, performing the pilgrimage (*ḥajj*) to Mecca, es-

At the age of five, he began studying and memorizing the Qur'ān with the principal reciters. At age seven, he began studying Urdu and Persian, as well as mathematics, with the great scholar and author, Mawlānā Muḥammad Yāsīn, the father of Mawlānā Muftī Muḥammad Shāfiᶜ ᶜUthmānī.[3] Later, he studied the various Islamic sciences with the foremost scholars of India under the direct guidance and supervision of his uncle, Imām Ashraf ᶜAlī al-Thānawī.[4] He gave particular emphasis to Sacred Law (*fiqh*) and ḥadīth studies, became highly proficient in both, and distinguished above other students by his intellectual ability, and the benefit of his great uncle's tutelage.

After gaining his authorization (*ijāza*)[5] in the Islamic sciences, he moved to Saharanpur and attended the ḥadīth classes of the knower of Allāh, ḥadīth master and jurist, Mawlānā Khalīl Aḥmad al-Sahāranpūrī.[6] Following a period of close study with this great scholar, Mawlānā Ẓafar ᶜUthmānī received the Certificate of Completion in Higher Studies in 1328 AH, when he was 18; a certificate only awarded the most brilliant students at such a young age.

Given Mawlānā Ẓafar ᶜUthmānī's talent and intellectual skill, he was appointed teacher at the *madrasa* in Saharanpur. There he remained for seven years, teaching Sacred Law, fundamentals of jurisprudence (*uṣūl*), logic, and philosophy. He then moved to Madrasa

---

pecially from far lands like India, was a notable feat, requiring great physical and financial sacrifice; and the journey was a dangerous one.

3 Mawlānā Muḥammad Shāfiᶜ ᶜUthmānī (1314–1396 AH), known as *al-Muftī al-Aᶜẓam*, "the Grand Muftī," was one of the greatest scholars of the Indian Subcontinent. He is the father of Muftī Taqī ᶜUthmānī, one of the top scholars of our age, especially known for his research in Islamic law, finance, and contemporary issues (*Aḥkām al-Qur'ān* 3:1–3).

4 Mawlānā Ashraf ᶜAlī al-Thānawī (1280–1362 AH) was known as *Ḥakīm al-Umma*, "the Wise Man of the Community." He authored over a thousand titles, and was revered as a great scholar and Sufi.

5 The authorization (*ijāza*) is a permission to teach the subjects studied, and gives the one who possesses it a contiguous chain (*sanad*) back to the authors of the books studied, and from them to the Prophet ﷺ, the source of all sacred knowledge.

6 Mawlānā Khalīl Aḥmad al-Sahāranpūrī was the author of *Badhl al-Majhūd fī Sharḥ Sunan Abī Dāwūd*, a monumental commentary on the *Sunan* of Imām Abū Dāwūd, one of the six main collections of ḥadīth.

Imdād al-ʿUlūm in Thānā Bhāwan, where he taught all the ḥadīth works on the curriculum.[7] He also taught Qur'ānic exegesis. Being a gifted teacher, a vast number of distinguished scholars graduated under his guidance, and went on to spread sacred knowledge in the lands.

At this point, Imām Ashraf ʿAlī al-Thānawī commissioned him to write *Iʿlā' al-Sunan*, answer legal questions, and teach in his stead.[8] It took Imām Ẓafar roughly twenty years to author the eighteen large volumes of the *Iʿlā' al-Sunan*. He also wrote a two-volume preface and added a volume in which he compiled detailed biographies of Imām Abū Ḥanīfa, his students, and the scholars of the Ḥanafī school, limiting himself to the jurists who were recognized ḥadīth specialists.

He wrote many other great works, both in Arabic and Urdu. These include a large collection of legal verdicts (*fatāwā*), *Aḥkām al-Qur'ān*, and a legal exegesis (*tafsīr*) of the Qur'ān in praise of which scholars and jurists said, "Reading it is a lasting blessing; authoring it is like a tremendous feat (*fatḥ*)."

When the subcontinent gained independence and India was divided, he moved to Pakistan and became head-teacher at Dār al-ʿUlūm, Hyderabad, Sind, benefiting students with his speech, spiritual state, and righteous works.

During the last years of his life, he remained constant in his remembrance and invocations, despite weak health and sickness. He performed all obligatory prayers in the mosque even though this required extreme physical exertion. In the month of Ramaḍān, 1394 AH, he fell very ill and doctors forbade him from fasting. He turned down their advice, saying, "Our master ʿAbbās ﷺ did not leave fasting when he was ninety, and would undergo many hardships to be able to fast." Allāh took his soul that very year. May Allāh be well pleased with him.

---

7 In the Indian Subcontinent, these are the following ḥadīth collections: *Ṣaḥīḥ al-Bukhārī, Muslim, Sunan Abī Dāwūd, Tirmidhī, Nasā'ī, Ibn Māja*, and Tabrīzī's *Miskhāt al-Maṣābīḥ*.

8 This was a most noble distinction, as Imām Ashraf ʿAlī al-Thānawī was the most famous scholar of India at the time.

*Prophetic Guidance on the Spiritual Path*

# The Book of Sufism

As the object of this book [*Iʿlā' al-Sunan*] is to counter the charges of the literalists[1] against Ḥanafī scholars, we chose to close with something in reply to their accusations against Sufi scholars as well. For the literalists speak ill of them and claim that their way has no basis in the Qur'ān and Sunna. This belief arises from ignorance of the reality of Sufism, and from being affected by the practices and customs of ignorant would-be Sufis of our times. Had they but returned to the books of the Sufis, they would have known that the truth is with Allāh and His friends (*awliyā'*),[2] and their lies would have come to naught.

Sufism means drawing nearer to Allāh through knowledge and action. Thus, the Sufi is the one drawn near. Today, in the Islamic lands, this title is generally applied not to the one drawn near to

---

1 The literalists are those who stick to their own, narrow understanding of the Qur'ān and Sunna, without accepting the interpretative frameworks set down by the scholars of Sacred Law. In the Indian Subcontinent, they were critical of the Ḥanafī School, and claimed it was far from the primary texts. It was in response to such accusations that Imām Ẓafar ʿUthmānī authored his work, which contains over 6123 ḥadīths, and copious commentary, as proofs for the soundness of the positions of the Ḥanafī School, which remains the largest of the four orthodox schools of Sacred Law.

2 In his commentary on Imām Qushayrī's *Risāla* Shaykh al-Islām Zakariyyā al-Anṣārī explains that "electhood (*wilāya*) is general and specific. As for general electhood, it is to carry out what one was commanded to do [by Allāh]. The specific electhood is Allāh's love and protection of the slave" (*Sharḥ al-Risāla al-Qushayrīyya* 3:207).

Allāh, but rather to those who cling to certain outward manners and forms.[3] Moreover, how many people close to Allāh in the lands are not known as Sufis, simply because they do not adorn themselves in the garb of the Sufis?

Sufism is a branch of the Sacred Law (*fiqh*), since the Sacred Law entails knowing the self, and what is for it and against it, as is reported from Abū Ḥanīfa (may Allāh have mercy on him). It is clear that knowing the way to draw closer to Allāh through knowledge and works is not only part of Sacred Law—it is the very essence of Sacred Law.[4] Thus, the jurist (*faqīh*) is he who has drawn near to Allāh by knowledge coupled with actions, not merely by the knowledge of legal rulings and their proofs. Such a jurist is what is meant by the Prophet's ﷺ words: "A single jurist is harder on Satan than a thousand worshippers" (*Tirmidhī* and *Ibn Māja*). That is the jurist who acts upon his knowledge of Sacred Law, and draws near to Allāh through his knowledge and actions. Allāh Most High says, "Only the knowledgeable of Allāh's servants fear Him" (Qur'ān 35:28). He says, "Only the knowledgeable" thereby negating the possibility of [true] knowledge and deep understanding (*fiqh*) for those who do not fear Allāh. It thus became clear to scholars who seek the next life that the path to divine knowledge and stations of proximity is closed off except to those who possess renunciation (*zuhd*)[5] and piety (*taqwā*). Hence, through piety and high levels of renunciation does a servant

---

3 The author is making a general statement, for the exceptions are plenty. His very own uncle and spiritual guide, Imām Ashraf ʿAlī al-Thānawī, for example, was famous as a Sufi.

4 The great knower of Allāh, Imām Aḥmad al-Rifāʿī (Allāh be pleased with him) explained that, "The spiritual path (*ṭarīq*) is to say, 'I believe in Allāh, stand fast to the limits of Allāh, exalt that which Allāh exalts, and avoid that which Allāh forbade.' There is no spiritual path beyond this, for there is nothing beyond guidance except misguidance" (*Kitāb Kashf al-Asrār li Tanwīr al-Abṣār* 73).

5 Renunciation (*zuhd*) is to content oneself with the necessary amount of that which is without doubt known to be lawful (*ḥalāl*). Higher than this is the renunciation of those brought close to Allāh (*muqarrabīn*), for it is renunciation of all other than Allāh Most High, whether in this world, the Garden or anywhere else. One who has such renunciation has no goal but reaching Allāh and being close to Him, and makes all his other goals subservient to these (*Kashshāf Iṣṭilāḥāt al-Funūn* 1:913).

become immersed in both knowledge and action. This is the essence of Sufism. The one who realizes this is a true Sufi.

So I ask you, by Allāh, is there any innovation (*bidʿa*) in this? Has this no basis in the Sacred Law? Nay, it is the essence of Sacred Law and the very purpose of all sacred rulings.[6] Ibn Masʿūd ﷺ said, "Knowledge is not [merely] the narrating of texts. Rather, knowledge is fear [of Allāh]."

Hence, Sufism is entirely manners (*ādāb*). Every time, state, and station has its manners. Therefore, whoever adheres to the manners of each moment shall reach the stations of the accomplished Sufis. And whoever strays from manners and proper conduct is far from the proximity he thinks he enjoys, and is rejected when he thinks he is accepted. Abū Ḥafs (may Allāh have mercy on him) said, "Outward manners are the sign of inward demeanor," for the Prophet ﷺ said, "Had his heart been reverent (*khashāʿa*), his limbs would have been reverent" (*Ḥakīm al-Tirmidhī*, with a weak chain of narrators; it is also related from the words of Saʿīd ibn al-Musayyib in *Muṣannaf ʿAbd al-Razzāq*). When Abū Muḥammad al-Ḥarīrī was asked about Sufism, he replied, "It is entering into every high trait, and leaving every low trait," as mentioned in Suhrawardī's *Maʿārif*.

In short, Sufism gives life to both the outward and inward. As for the outward, it does so through good deeds. As for the inward, it does so through the remembrance of Allāh, leaving reliance on other than Him, adorning oneself with praiseworthy traits (*akhlāq*), and purifying oneself of the taint of base traits. This was possible for the early Muslims (*salaf*) merely through keeping good company, just as knowledge of the Book of Allāh and the Prophetic Sunna was gained in this way without the need for books and the sciences recorded in them. Then, when the situation changed, it became necessary to record the sciences, to compile and transmit them, and to build centers of learning to teach these recorded sciences. Likewise, when the Sufis saw the change in people's condition, they introduced spiritual exercises

6 This is why scholars defined the spiritual path as being "nothing but performing the spiritual works of the Sacred Law" (*Kitāb Kashf al-Asrār li Tanwīr al-Abṣār* 73).

and retreats to develop the outward and inward, and they built Sufi hostels (*zāwiyas*) and centers. It is clear that these are all mere means, as [the recording and systemization of] the Islamic sciences, and the goals [of Sufism] are firmly established by texts of the Book of Allāh, the Sunna, and the sayings of the Companions and the Followers (*tābiᶜīn*).[7] Whoever intently studies the chapters on good manners (*ādāb*), renunciation (*zuhd*), and softening the heart (*raqā'iq*) in the books of ḥadīth will know that this is the very essence of Sufism, but the people of the outward[8] do not understand.

Henceforth, know that goodness in one's social dealings (*ḥusn al-muᶜāshara maᶜa 'l-khalq*) is part of developing the outward, though most people—even the scholars—are negligent of it. Rather, they have reduced the development of the outward to the acts of worship such as prayer, fasting, *zakāt*, and the pilgrimage; and left goodness in social dealings behind them. This has become a widespread problem (*fitna*) dividing the hearts of the Muslims after they had been together and united. And tribulation has appeared on land and sea because of it.[9]

How can goodness in social dealings not be a religious duty, when the Lawgiver has commanded it, just as He has commanded the acts of worship, and He commanded them both equally? Do you not grasp the saying of the Prophet ﷺ, "None of you [truly] believes until he loves for his brother what he loves for himself?" (*Bukhārī* and *Muslim*). And when he ﷺ was asked about righteousness, he said, "Righteousness is good character" (*Muslim, Tirmidhī,* and *Aḥmad*). He also said, "If you are three, then let not two of you converse without the third, for that saddens him" (*Bukhārī* and *Muslim*).

So, if Allāh, the One, does not approve of a Muslim being sad-

---

7 A Follower (*tābiᶜī*) is, "Someone who met a Companion of the Prophet ﷺ while believing in the [messengerhood of] the Prophet ﷺ and died a Muslim" (*Kashshāf Iṣṭilāḥāt al-Funūn* 1:362).

8 The author intends by "the people of the outward," those who see Islām as mere outward forms, and ignore its inner realities; not the scholars of the outward—of whom he was a most noble example.

9 This is taken from the Qur'ānic verse: "Corruption appears on land and sea because of [the evil] which men's hands have done" (Qur'ān 30: 41).

dened by the likes of this—and many do not pay attention to such matters—how, then, can He approve of things worse than this that sadden them?

The basis of being good in social dealings is seeking to make your fellow believer happy.[10] This is one of the greatest of the works of the noble Sufis. So observe, then, who it is that acts upon the Book of Allāh and the Sunna, and who is wading in the seas of ignorance, innovation, and sin.

**The Ḥadīths**

1. Nawwās ibn Samᶜān ﷺ reported that

> I asked the Messenger of Allāh ﷺ about righteousness (*birr*) and sin. He replied, "Righteousness is good character, and sin is that which wavers in your soul and you loathe to have people uncover" (*Muslim*).

[Kumushkhānawī comments:

"Righteousness" is pleasing action. This ḥadīth is of the comprehensive speech (*jawāmiᶜ al-kalim*) of the Prophet ﷺ, for righteousness (*birr*) is a word that encompasses all good, and sin (*ithm*) encompasses all evil (*Lawāmiᶜ al-ᶜUqūl* 2:358).

Mullā ᶜAlī al-Qārī adds:

Righteousness with the Creator means busying oneself with all obligatory and voluntary actions, and performing praiseworthy deeds while knowing that all one does is deficient and in need of pardon, while all that Allāh does is perfect and deserves thanks. . . . . After this, one adorns oneself with the traits of Allāh at all times by continually turning away from all other than Him, while always directing oneself to Him and remaining constant in His remembrance (*Mirqāt al-Mafātīḥ* 8:803–4).]

10 Our master ᶜUmar ﷺ reported that the Messenger of Allāh ﷺ said, "The best of actions is to bring happiness to the heart of the believer" (*Ṭabarānī* and others).

2. Abū Hurayra ﷺ reported that the Messenger of Allāh ﷺ said,

   Look at those below you, and look not at those above you, for it is closer to not denying the blessings of Allāh upon you (*Bukhārī* and *Muslim*).

3. Abū Hurayra ﷺ reported that the Messenger of Allāh ﷺ said,

   The rights a Muslim owes a Muslim are six: if you see him, greet him; if he invites you, accept his invitation; if he seeks your advice, advise him; if he sneezes and praises Allāh,[11] ask Allāh to have mercy on him; if he falls ill, visit him; and if he dies, attend his funeral (*Muslim*).

4. It is reported by Ibn Masʿūd ﷺ that the Messenger of Allāh ﷺ said,

   If you are three, let not two of you converse without including the third, until others join you, for that saddens the third one (*Bukhārī* and *Muslim;* the words are from Muslim's narration).

5. Ibn ʿUmar ﷺ reported that the Messenger of Allāh ﷺ said,

   One should not make another rise from his seat. Rather, spread out and make room (*Bukhārī* and *Muslim*).

6. ʿAmr ibn Shuʿayb relates from his father, who relates from his grandfather that the Messenger of Allāh ﷺ said,

   Eat, drink, dress well, and give in charity, without excess or conceit (*Bukhārī, Abū Dāwūd,* and *Aḥmad*).

[Mullā ʿAlī al-Qārī comments:

In [Imām al-Ghazālī's] *Minhāj al-ʿĀbidīn* it is mentioned that Farqad al-Sinjī entered in rags upon Ḥasan [al-Baṣrī] while the latter was wearing fine garments. Farqad began [self-consciously] touching his

---

11 The one who sneezes says *Al-ḥamdu li 'Llāh* (Praise be to Allāh). The one who hears must say, "*Yarḥamuk Allāh*" (May Allāh have mercy upon you).

rags so Ḥasan said, "Why look you thus at my garments? They are the garments of the people of the Garden. And your rags are the garments of the people of the Fire. It has reached me that most of the people of the Fire wear rags." Then he added, "They [the people of the Fire] limited renunciation (*zuhd*) to their clothing and left arrogance (*kibr*) in their hearts."

This [to dress well] is the chosen practice of the Naqshabandīs, Shādhilīs, and Bakrīs, for they did not limit themselves to any particular dress . . . unlike certain other Sufis. May Allāh benefit us by their *baraka* and their good intentions (*Mirqāt al-Mafātīḥ* 8:175).]

7. Abū Hurayra ﵁ reported that the Messenger of Allāh ﷺ said,

> Whoever desires that Allāh increase his provision and extend his life, let him maintain his family ties (*Bukhārī*).

[Mullā ʿAlī al-Qārī comments:

To "maintain family ties" means to be good, loving, and gentle toward one's kin, while keeping track of how they are doing [to learn if they need help or are facing difficulties] (*Mirqāt al-Mafātīḥ* 8:647).]

8. Jubayr ibn Muṭʿim ﵁ reported that the Messenger of Allāh ﷺ said,

> One who severs [family ties] shall not enter the Garden (*Bukhārī* and *Muslim*).

[Kumushkhānawī comments:

"Shall not enter the Garden," that is, with those who enter first without punishment or trouble, and will not enter it until punished for what he did. Tawrīshī said: "This is the way to understand such ḥadīths [that outwardly indicate that a believer may abide in the Fire for a sin, for the Sunnī understanding is that all believers will, in the end, enter the Garden], as this corresponds to the principles of the religion. The vast majority of the innovators have perished by holding fast to the outward purport of such texts, but anyone who understands the way of expression and meanings of the speech of the Arabs can, with the assistance of Allāh, easily comprehend such reported texts" (*Lawāmiᶜ al-ᶜUqūl* 5:139).]

9. Mughīra ibn Shuᶜba ﷺ reported that the Messenger of Allāh ﷺ said,

> Allāh forbids that you treat your mothers badly; that you kill your baby daughters; or not give while asking others. He dislikes that you talk needlessly, ask too many questions, or waste money (*Bukhārī* and *Muslim*).

[Qārī comments:

"Allāh forbids that you treat your mothers badly," means that one does not disobey them nor is one rude to them, such that one does that which either parent dislikes, whether in action or speech. "He dislikes that you talk needlessly," has several possible interpretations. In the *Fā'iq* [by Zamakhsharī], it is explained as being a prohibition of the useless talk of those who sit together. Others explained it as including in it a prohibition of tale bearing and backbiting. Suyūṭī explained that what is meant is excess talk, for it leads to mistakes. "Ask too many questions": this too has several explanations. Asking about the affairs of people and prying into them excessively; or asking people for money; or excessive questioning in issues of knowledge, in order to test the one questioned or to show off; or asking without need" (*Mirqāt al-Mafātīḥ* 8:651–2).]

10. Anas ﷺ reported that the Prophet ﷺ said,

> By the One in whose Hand is my soul, no servant [of Allāh] believes until he loves for his neighbor and brother what he loves for himself (*Bukhārī* and *Muslim*).

[Kumushkhānawī comments:

"By the one in whose hand," i.e., under whose power and disposal, "is my soul," i.e., my entity and existence, "no servant [of Allāh]," wholly and truly "believes until he loves for his neighbor and brother what he loves for himself" (*Lawāmiᶜ al-ᶜUqūl* 4:695, 713).

Qārī comments:

The believers are one in soul though many in body—like a single light in differing manifestations, or a single soul in different bodies, such that if one is hurt, all are affected. This meaning is indicated by the Prophet's ﷺ saying, "The believers are like a single man. If his eye hurts, his whole body hurts. And if his head hurts, his whole body hurts." It is reported from one of the *shaykhs* of the Naqshabandī path that he [all at once] began to feel cold and said, "Cover me! Cover me!" So his students covered him. Then came a disciple of his who had fallen into cold water on a chilly winter day. The *shaykh* told them, "Warm him up." When the disciple began to feel warmer so did the *shaykh*. Similar to it is [the story that] once Laylā began to bleed and blood came out of [Majnūn] al-ᶜĀmirī's hand as he sang,

> I am the lover, and the one I love is me
> We are two souls that reside in one body.

This is so because [in the case of true believers] their faith is . . . in reality, from the light of Allāh, which is the light of Divine Oneness (*tawḥīd*), from the reflection of the light of Solitude (*fardāniyya*), from the light of the Entity of Allāh. Their souls are united by that light, leading to fondness and mercy (*Mirqāt al-Mafātīḥ* 8:697).]

11. It is reported by Abū Ayyūb ﷺ that Allāh's Messenger ﷺ said,

> It is forbidden for a believer to avoid his fellow brother for more than three days, such that when they meet, each ignores the other. And the one who gives the *salām* first is the better of the two[12] (*Bukhārī* and *Muslim*).

---

12 Abū 'l-Dardā' reported that the Messenger of Allāh ﷺ said, "Should I not inform you of something higher in rank than fasting, charity, and prayer?" We said, "Yes!" He said, "Mending relationships; and destroying relationships is the destroyer" (*Abu Dāwūd* and *Tirmidhī*, who said it is rigorously authentic).

# Renunciation & Scrupulousness

12. Nuʿmān ibn Bashīr ﷺ reported that he heard the Messenger of Allāh ﷺ say,

> The lawful is plain, and the unlawful is plain. Between them are doubtful matters that most people do not know about. He who avoids the doubtful has kept his religion and honor clear. But he who falls into the doubtful falls into the unlawful as the shepherd who grazes around a sanctuary, almost grazing therein. Verily, every king has a sanctuary. Verily, Allāh's sanctuary is His prohibitions. Verily, there is a morsel of flesh in the body which, if sound, the whole body is sound, and which, if ill, the whole body is ill. Verily, it is the heart (*Bukhārī* and *Muslim*).

Imām Ẓafar ʿUthmānī himself comments:

The Imāms agree unanimously upon the tremendous importance of this ḥadīth, for it is one of the ḥadīths around which the foundational concepts of Islām revolve. The reality of scrupulousness (*waraʿ*)[13] is explained by the Prophet ﷺ saying, "He who avoids the doubtful

13 "Scrupulousness is defined by spiritual travelers (*sālikīn*) as leaving everything doubt-

has kept his religion and honor clear," and this is not possible except through renunciation of worldly matters (*dunyā*) and dedication to the next life. For this reason, he ﷺ followed it by saying, "Verily, there is a morsel of flesh in the body. . . ." This indicates that scrupulousness is not possible except by possessing a sound heart and its being purified of the love of the worldly, for love of the worldly is the root of all error. It is well known that renunciation (*zuhd*) is the first step of the noble Sufis on the path of drawing near to Allāh, and they are the people most avidly concerned with renunciation. Knowing that renunciation is not possible except in a sound heart, they engage in the most intense of spiritual struggles until they attain unto it and thereby reach their desired goal.

[Kumushkhānawī comments:

"The lawful is plain"—that is, clear and its lawfulness is apparent—"and the unlawful is plain. Between them are doubtful matters." These are unclear as to whether they are lawful or prohibited due to conflicting proofs or meanings "that most people do not know about." Rather, only a few know about their ruling, and they are those firm-footed in their knowledge. But if the evidence is probabilistic, open to the possibility of unlawfulness, then it is of scrupulousness to leave it, as he indicated: "He who avoids the doubtful." "Avoid" (*ittaqā*) is from [the same linguistic root as] *taqwā* (piety), which linguistically means, "placing a shield or barrier around the self." In the context of the Sacred Law, it means protecting the self from sins and whatever leads to them. According to the Sufis, it is to divest oneself of all besides Allāh. This root meaning indicates that leaving the doubtful is only worthy of consideration in keeping one's religion and honor clear if it is free of the likes of ostentation (*riyā'*). "Has kept his religion and honor clear. But he who falls into the doubtful falls into the unlawful," that is, it is feared that he will fall into it, for he is encircling it "as the shepherd

ful, and taking oneself to account (*muḥāsaba*) every moment" (*Kashshāf Iṣṭilāḥāt al-Funūn* 2:1777–8).

who grazes around a sanctuary, almost grazing therein. Verily, every king has a sanctuary," which none is allowed to enter and is warned from approaching by the sternest of punishments. "Verily, Allāh's sanctuary is His prohibitions." Thus, the one who is careful about his religion does not come close to that which could lead to error. The central purpose of this ḥadīth is to establish a clear proof for the leaving of doubtful matters. As scrupulousness (*wara*ʿ) inclines the heart toward righteousness, and the lack of it [inclines the heart] toward sin, he said: "Verily, there is a morsel of flesh in the body"—though small in size is tremendous in worth—"which, if sound," by having been expanded by guidance, "the whole body is sound." And is thus used in acts of obedience, for the limbs are subservient [to the heart], "which, if ill," and darkened by misguidance, "the whole body is ill," from having been used in despicable acts. "Verily, it is the heart." This ḥadīth has a tremendous place in the Sacred Law, and it is from the light of Prophethood (*Lawāmi*ʿ *al-*ʿ*Uqūl* 2: 425-6).]

13. Abū Hurayra ﷺ reported that the Messenger of Allāh ﷺ said,

> Wretched is the slave to *dirhams* and *dinārs* and lavish clothing. If given, he is content; if not, he is not (*Bukhārī*).

Imām Ẓafar ʿUthmānī comments:

The Prophet's ﷺ saying, "Wretched is the slave to *dirhams* and *dinārs*," is similar to Allāh's saying, "And among mankind is he who worships Allāh upon a narrow brink, so that if good befalls him he is content therewith, but if a trial befalls him, he falls away utterly. [He loses both the world and the Hereafter. That is the sheer loss]" (Qur'ān, 22:11). By "the slave to *dirhams* and *dīnārs*," the Prophet ﷺ meant those whom the worldly life has imprisoned by its demands, until they become as slaves to it, and it deals with them as a master. And whoever is a slave to his whims is not honest when he says, "Thee (alone) we worship; Thee (alone) we ask for help" (Qur'ān, 1:4). Curbing whims, avarice, and greed is the first step of the people of renunciation (*zāhidīn*), and the noble Sufis are the most concerned of people regarding this.

And whoever curbs his whims will "be in the world as a stranger, or a passer-by."

[Qārī comments:

"Wretched is the slave to *dirhams* and *dīnārs*," who has made these his pleasure and his mighty lord by acquiring it wrongly and not spending it as is fitting. They have been specified for mention, as they are the means through which all the desires of the lower self and Satan are fulfilled. "And lavish clothing": the general case is for them to be worn out of vanity, pride and ostentation. "Be in the world as though a stranger. . ." Imām Nawawī (may Allāh have mercy on him) explained, "Do not incline toward the world and do not make it your [final] abode. Do not be attached to it, except as a stranger is in a strange land." This is because the world is an abode meant to be traversed, a bridge to be crossed. Therefore, it is incumbent on the believer to busy himself with acts of worship and obedience, and to await his journeying-on . . . not to busy himself with that which does not concern him of vain hopes and great avarice. "Or a passer-by," that is, a passer-by on the road; this is more emphatic than being a stranger, for a stranger could make a strange land his residence, and live there a while (*Mirqāt al-Mafātīḥ* 9: 11, 125-6).]

14. Ibn ᶜUmar ﷺ reported that the Messenger of Allāh ﷺ took me by the shoulders and said,

> Be in the world as though a stranger or a passer-by.

Ibn ᶜUmar used to say,

> In the evening, do not wait for morning, and in the morning, do not wait for evening. Take from your health for your weakness; and from your life for your death (*Bukhārī*).

15. Ibn ᶜUmar ﷺ also reported that the Messenger of Allāh ﷺ said,

> Whoever imitates a people is of them (*Abū Dāwūd* and *Ibn Ḥibbān*; it is rigorously authenticated).

Imām Ẓafar ʿUthmānī comments:

In the Prophet's ﷺ saying, "Whoever imitates a people is of them," there is praise for those who imitate the people of renunciation (*zāhidīn*) with sincere intention, without pretense or show. It may well be that he will become of them, and realize their spiritual states.

[Qārī comments:

"Whoever imitates a people," i.e. whoever imitates the non-Muslims, corrupt or sinful, in dress [and appearance], for example, or imitates the people of Sufism and foremost of the righteous, "is of them," in sin or good. . . [And it is well known that] the Beloved does not punish one like His beloved (*Mirqāt al-Mafātīḥ* 8:155).]

16. Ibn ʿAbbās ﷺ said that,

> I was behind the Prophet ﷺ one day, when he said, "O youth! Be mindful of Allāh and He will be mindful of you. Be mindful of Allāh and you will find Him before you. If you ask, ask Allāh, and if you rely, rely on Allāh" (*Tirmidhī*; it is good and well authenticated).

Imām Ẓafar ʿUthmānī comments:

In the Prophet's ﷺ saying, "O youth! Be mindful of Allāh and He will be mindful of you," there is clear confirmation of the Sufis' spiritual vigilance (*murāqaba*) of the tremendousness of Allāh, and their perpetual guarding of this in their hearts. In his saying "Be mindful of Allāh and you will find Him before you" is clear indication of the attainment of spiritual beholding (*mushāhada*) after vigilant observation (*murāqaba*). This spiritual beholding is among the highest goals of the Sufis.

[Qārī comments:

"O youth! Be mindful of Allāh," in His commands and prohibitions, "and He will be mindful of you." That is, He will protect you in your worldly life from hardships and disliked matters, and in the next life from punishment . . . for whoever is for Allāh, Allāh is with him. "Be mindful of Allāh," that is, be mindful of His rights by constantly remembering Him, and being continual in your contemplation and thanks of Him, and you will behold Him in your stations of spiritual excellence, certainty, and perfect faith. It will be as though you see Him, such that you are completely annihilated from seeing any besides Him. Thus, the first part [of this ḥadīth] is spiritual vigilance (*murāqaba*); the second is spiritual beholding (*mushāhada*). . . . In it there is an allusion to His saying, "We are nearer to him than his jugular vein" (Qur'ān 50:16). Some of the knowers of Allāh (*ʿārifīn*) indicated that there is no atom of the atoms of this world except that the Light of Lights encompasses it, and has overwhelming mastery over it, being closer to it than its own being, not just by knowledge alone, nor by creation alone, but, rather, in a sense that [is so subtle it] cannot be disclosed. "If you ask, ask Allāh, and if you rely, rely on Allāh." For every blessing and succor, whether worldly or other, only reaches the slave or is averted from him by His Mercy, without any need or cause. He is the Absolutely Generous, the Wealthy who is without need. Thus, it is only befitting that only His Mercy be hoped for; that only His Vengeance be feared; that He be turned to in all matters; and that none other be asked, for they are unable to give or take, benefit or harm. . . . And one should never leave asking Allāh, whether by tongue or state. . . for in asking is a manifestation of the signs of humility, an admission of helplessness and need, and the lack of all ability and power (*Mirqāt al-Mafātīḥ* 9:163).]

17. Sahl ibn Saʿd ﷺ reported that

> A man came to the Prophet ﷺ and asked, "O Messenger of Allāh, guide me to an action through which both Allāh and people will love me." He said, "Renounce the worldly and Allāh will love you; renounce what people have and they will love you" (*Ibn Māja* and others with a sound chain).

18. Saʿd ibn Abī Waqqās ﷺ relates the above ḥadīth with the words:

He said, "Counsel me," so [the Messenger of Allāh ﷺ] replied, "Despair of that which is in the hands of people, and beware of avarice (*ṭamaʿ*) for it is instant poverty" (*Bayhaqī* and *Ḥākim*; it is rigorously authenticated).

19. Saʿd ibn Abī Waqqās ؓ reported that,

I heard the Messenger of Allāh ﷺ say, "Verily, Allāh loves the god-fearing , rich, unknown servant" (*Muslim*).

20. Abū Hurayra ؓ reported that the Messenger of Allāh ﷺ said,

From the excellence of a man's Islam is leaving that which does not concern him" (*Tirmidhī*. it is sound).

[Qārī comments:

"From the excellence of a man's Islam is leaving that which does not concern him." That is, to leave that which is not important or befitting of him, whether of speech, action, or thought. Thus, "the excellence of a man's Islam" is its perfection, such that one remains steadfast in the submission to the commands and prohibitions of Allāh, and surrenders to His rulings in accordance to His destiny and decree. This is the sign of the heart expanded by the light of its Lord, and the descent of quietude (*sakīna*) into the heart. The reality of "that which does not concern him" is that which is not a worldly or next-worldly necessity, and does not aide in attaining his Lord's good pleasure; that which is possible to live without. This includes excess acts and unnecessary speech. This ḥadīth may well be taken from Allāh Most High's saying, "And who shun all vain things" (Qur'ān 23:3). And it has been related in a prophetic ḥadīth that, "The people of the Garden will regret naught but moments that passed them by without remembrance of Allāh" (*Ṭabarānī* from our master Muʿādh ؓ). So glad tidings to one who takes himself to account before he is taken to account. Allāh Most High has said, "O you who believe! Observe your duty to Allāh. And let every soul look to that which it sends on before for the morrow. And observe your duty to Allāh! Lo! Allāh is informed of what you do. And be you not as those who forgot Allāh, therefore He caused them to forget their souls. Such are the evil-doers" (Qur'ān 59:18–19). Al-Awzāʿī said, "[The righteous caliph] ʿUmar ibn ʿAbd al-ʿAzīz wrote to us: 'Whoever remembers death often is content with but a little of this world. And whoever considers his speech to be of his actions speaks little except for that which benefits him'" (*Mirqāt al-Mafātīḥ* 8:585).]

Imām Ẓafar ʿUthmānī comments:

In the Prophet's ﷺ saying "From the excellence of a man's Islam is leaving that which does not concern him" is an indication of the way to achieve the spiritual excellence (*iḥsān*) mentioned in the Jibrīl Ḥadīth by the Prophet's ﷺ saying, "To worship Allāh as though you see Him, and if you see Him not, then [know that] He sees you." For the excellence of a man's Islam is attaining unto this spiritual excellence. Thus, whoever beholds in his heart that Allāh Most High observes the actions of the servant, is aware of his speech, and knows his condition, such a person's words and speech in other than that which concerns him will be scant. Thus, this ḥadīth is from the comprehensive words of Prophetic speech, and is a foundation of the pristine, lofty way of the Sufis.

21. Anas ﷺ reported that the Messenger of Allāh ﷺ said,

> All the children of Adam err, and the best of those who err are the oft-repenting (*Tirmidhī*, and *Ibn Māja*, with a strong chain).

Imām Ẓafar ʿUthmānī comments:

In the Prophet's ﷺ saying "All the children of Adam err, and the best of those who err are the oft-repenting" is, for the god-fearing who perform good works, a deterrent from feeling conceited about these works, or thinking highly of themselves. For, apart from the Prophets and Messengers, the servant of Allāh is never inviolably protected (*maʿṣūm*) from error, even if he attains the limits of spiritual union and nearness. As for them [the Prophets and Messengers], the Community is in unanimous agreement that they are inviolably protected from sins, whether intentional or unintentional. Others, however, have no such inviolable protection. Thus, they cannot be heedless of repentance, even for a moment. [They are ever] turning to their Lord, and seeking forgiveness for their sins. How could they do otherwise when the Messenger of Allāh ﷺ used to seek forgiveness from Allāh and repent to Him seventy times a day? Repentance is of the first and last stages of Sufism.

22. Anas  reported that the Messenger of Allāh ﷺ said,

> Silence is wisdom, though few are silent (*Bayhaqī*, with a weak chain; he deemed it to be the words of Luqmān the Wise).

Imām Ẓafar ʿUthmānī comments:

"Silence is wisdom, though few are silent," is a confirmation of the practices of the Sufis, for limiting speech is among the spiritual struggles (*mujāhada*) upon which they built their way. There are several prophetic ḥadīths in praise of silence in place of unnecessary speech. Among them is the ḥadīth of Ibn ʿUmar  that the Prophet ﷺ said, "Whoever is silent has attained salvation" (*Tirmidhī*, and *Ṭabarānī*, with a reliable chain). Muḥammad ibn al-Ḥasan reported at the end of his *Āthār*, from Abū Ḥanīfa, from Ḥammād, that Ibrāhīm [al-Nakhaʿī] said, "Tribulations are caused by speech." Qāḍī Ibn Bahlūl said, "Do not utter words you abhor for it may be that the tongue utters words and they come to be." Imām Mālik reports from Aslam that our master ʿUmar  came to our master Abū Bakr  one day while the latter was holding his tongue. ʿUmar said to him, "May Allāh forgive you!" Abū Bakr replied, "Verily this has cast me into (countless) troubles." And Imām Aḥmad, Nasāʾī, Ibn Māja, and Tirmidhī relate with a chain that Tirmidhī deemed good and well-authenticated, from Muʿādh ibn Jabal that he asked, "O Messenger of Allāh, are we taken to task for what we say?" He ﷺ said, "May your mother be bereaved of you,

O Muʿādh! Are people dragged into the Fire on their faces—or their noses—for anything but what their tongues have reaped?" Therefore, it is upon the intelligent person to be aware of his times, directed to what is of consequence, and wary of his tongue. And whoever considers his speech to be of his actions speaks little except for that which benefits him.

# Warning Against Base Character

THE WEAK servant of Allāh [Imām Ẓafar ʿUthmānī (may Allāh have mercy on him)] says:

Refining character traits (*tazkiya*) is one of the central concerns of the Sufis, for they consider noble traits to be stations on the spiritual path. They are distinguished from others by their good character, and through it they are known. Whoever examines the Qur'ān and Sunna with deliberation will know that good character is as central to religion as a foundation is to a building.

Improving character traits is not possible except through spiritual struggle at the hands of a perfected spiritual guide (*shaykh*)[14] who has

14 Imām Muḥammad ʿAlī al-Thānawī, who is not related to the author, warned that "When a seeker (*murīd*) thinks he has found a spiritual guide, it is incumbent upon him to be cautious and exert his utmost effort in finding out whether the guide is fit to be a shaykh or not. Many seekers have been misled and have perished in this area [by following would-be guides]; rather, most of humanity has been led astray and has perished by following misguided leaders. The proper way, then, is to carefully examine whether the spiritual guide is uprightly adhering to the Sacred Law (*Sharīʿa*), the [principles of the] spiritual way (*ṭarīqa*) and the higher realities (*ḥaqīqa*). If he is an innovator, this can be known by what [learned] people say about him, and by the conduct of those who follow and love him without correcting him. If the seeker

struggled with his own self, opposed his caprice, abandoned base character traits, and adorned himself with praiseworthy ones. Whoever thinks they can achieve this through mere knowledge and the study of books has erred and gone far astray. Just as (outward) knowledge is only acquired through study with scholars, good character is acquired by struggling to attain it at the hands of the knowers of Allāh.

Good character is an attribute of the Master of the Messengers ﷺ,[15] and the best of the works of the truthful (*ṣiddīqīn*), and is in reality half of religion. It is from the fruits of the spiritual struggles of the god-fearing, and the efforts of the worshippers. Base character is a lethal poison, a fatal destroyer, and a humiliating debaser—manifest vileness, and filth that distances one from the sanctuary of the Lord of the worlds. It makes the one characterized by it of the devils, and it is the open door to the burning fire of Allāh that "leaps up over the hearts (of men)" (Qur'ān 104:7). Good character, on the other hand, is the open door to the bounties of the Gardens and proximity to the Merciful. Base character is a sickness of the heart and a disease of the lower self. It is a sickness that endangers the ever-lasting life. Therefore, it is necessary to pay utmost attention to it, even more than outward sickness.

Character traits are attributes of the self by which it leans to either beauty or ugliness. Complete outward beauty is not possible through the beauty of the eyes alone, without the nose, mouth, and cheeks. Rather, it is necessary that all these be beautiful. Similarly, inward beauty requires four essential elements. And good character is completed through an appropriate balance and temperance of these

---

finds out that the scholars of the time are not critical of this spiritual guide, and that some scholars and notables, young or old, take him as a guide and turn to him in their search for the spiritual way and higher realities, then he will know that such a spiritual guide is worthy of being followed" (*Kashshāf Iṣṭilāḥāt al-Funūn* 1:1050).

15 Allāh Most High said of the Prophet ﷺ, "And lo! Thou art of a tremendous nature" (Qur'ān 68:4). Imām Junayd (may Allāh be pleased with him) explained that "His nature was tremendous because he had no desire but Allāh" (*Al-Barīqa al-Maḥmūdiyya fī Sharḥ al-Ṭarīqa al-Muḥammadīyya* 2:41).

elements. These elements are: knowledge, anger, passion, and justice between the other three elements.

As for the attribute of knowledge, its good and uprightness lies in its ability to comprehend the difference between truthfulness and treachery in speech, between truth and falsehood in belief, between good and evil in actions. If this attribute of knowledge is made upright, then its fruits are wisdom, which is at the root of good character. Allāh said of wisdom: "And he unto whom wisdom is given, he has truly received abundant good" (Qur'ān 2:269). And it is what the Prophet ﷺ meant by profound understanding (*fiqh*) when he said, "Whoever Allāh wishes good for, He gives profound understanding (*fiqh*) of religion" (*Bukhārī* and *Muslim*).

As for the attribute of anger, its good lies in its suppression, and its expression in accordance with the dictates of wisdom. Likewise, the good and uprightness of passion lies in its being under the guidance of wisdom: that is, the guidance of the intellect and Sacred Law.

Know, then, that those whom laziness has overcome find it difficult to carry out spiritual struggle, to discipline and purify the self, and to refine their character. They wrongly believe that because natures do not undergo change, it is not possible to change character traits. If this were the case, then counsel, admonition, and discipline would be of no use. How can it not be possible to change the behavior of humans, when it is clear that it is possible to change the behavior of animals such as eagles, dogs, and horses by training?

In reality, those who deny that character traits can be changed have confused changing traits with removing them. What is not possible is the second. If one sought to completely remove all traces of anger and passion, it would not be possible. However, it is possible to control and direct them through spiritual struggle and discipline, which we have been commanded to do, and these are the means of our salvation and the path to reach Allāh. At the same time, dispositions vary. Some are quick to change, others, slow.

How can it be desirable to uproot passion and anger completely when without anger, *jihād* would not be possible? How can it be a goal when the Prophets (Allāh bless them and give them peace) were characterized by them? For our Prophet ﷺ said, "I am a human, and I get angry as humans do" (*Aḥmad*, and *Muslim* with similar wording). Similarly, if someone spoke in his presence about a disliked matter, he would get so angry his cheeks would redden. However, he would not speak other than the truth, so his anger would not make him depart from the truth. Allāh Most High said, "Those who control their anger and are forgiving towards people; Allāh loves the good" (Qur'ān 3:134). Allāh did *not* say, "Those bereft of anger." Anger and passion are to be returned to a balanced state, such that they neither overcome nor master the intellect. Rather, the Sacred Law and intellect are to be the standards and masters over anger and passion. This is clearly possible, and is what changing character traits means. So, understand this.[16]

This balanced state is reached in two ways: by divine generosity and sound natural inclination, such that one is born with a high intellect and good character, and with passion and anger in balance. This is the case of the Prophets (Allāh bless them and give them peace). It is clearly conceivable that certain traits can be acquired through discipline, for it is very possible for a child to be honest, generous, and brave.

The other way to attain these noble traits is by spiritual struggle and discipline, namely, to make oneself perform the actions that a desired trait entails. These traits are then gradually acquired as one becomes used to those actions, as well as by keeping the company of those who already posses these traits.

One who wishes to become generous, for example, should force himself to act as a generous person would, by spending money. Then one constantly struggles with oneself by giving until it becomes naturally easy to give, and one becomes generous by nature. Likewise, one who wishes to become characterized by humility (*tawāḍuʿ*) after

16 At the end of noteworthy investigations, or after making a strong argument, it is the habit of scholars to say, "So understand" (*fa 'fham*). Out of good manners, if such texts are read to scholars, it is better to read, "So let it be understood" (*fa lyufham*), as the student must not command the teacher.

arrogance (*kibr*) was preponderant should force himself to perform the actions of the humble for a while, struggling with his lower self, until it becomes a character trait and these actions become easy. All traits that are praiseworthy in the Sacred Law may be attained by this means.

Keeping the company of perfected spiritual guides and avoiding the company of those with blameworthy traits has a strong effect, for dispositions (*ṭibāʿ*) can acquire good traits through company as it can acquire bad traits.[17] Moreover, for many people a *shaykh's* reminders and reprimands may achieve what mere determination and spiritual will may not. It may be that a student may leave the mire of base traits by the reminders and reprimands of his *shaykh* far more quickly than by his determination and spiritual will alone.[18]

If the self finds pleasure in habit and its usual companionship with the worthless, and inclines toward these, how can it not find pleasure in the worthwhile if it is returned to it for a period and is made to remain attached to it while mixing with the righteous and keeping their company and avoiding worthless company? In reality, the self's inclination towards despicable things is contrary to its natural disposition and akin to an inclination to eat dirt. As for its inclining to wisdom, the love and knowledge of Allāh, and His worship, it is like its inclination to food and drink. It is a result of the natural disposition of the heart, for the heart is a lordly matter.[19] Hence, the self's inclining to its passions is alien to it, and foreign to its disposition.

The food of hearts is wisdom, knowledge of Allāh, and love of Him.

---

17 With regard to this Shaykh ʿAbd al-Raḥmān al-Shāghūrī (may Allāh be pleased with him) would often mention the words of Allāh Most High: "O you who believe. Be mindful of your duty to Allāh, and be with the truthful" (Qur'ān 9:119).

18 At the same time, one must be highly cautious of false would-be Sufis. These are very common, and their most frequent sign is laxity (or, even more dangerous, complete disregard) towards the *Sharīʿa*. Sufis have long warned against such pretenders. Ramaḍān Effendī says, for example, "The most harmful of things to people are: keeping the company of a scholar who is heedless of Allāh or an ignorant Sufi" (*Sharḥ al-Ṭarīqa al-Muḥammadīyya* 1:31).

19 This alludes to Allāh Most High's saying, "They will ask you concerning the Spirit. Say: The Spirit is of the affair of my Lord" (Qur'ān 18:85).

The heart's turning away from its natural disposition is the result of illnesses that afflict it, as when an illness afflicts a person's stomach, causing him not to desire food or drink though they are the means for his survival. Accordingly, every heart that inclines to love of other than Allāh has a sickness to the extent of its inclination. The only exception is if it loved that thing as a means to the love of Allāh and His religion. This is subtle, however, and only known by those of spiritual insight. The opinion of the one afflicted is of little consequence in this, unless confirmed by his spiritual guide.

It is clear, then, that to acquire good character traits by spiritual discipline is certainly possible: by forcing oneself to perform certain actions until they become a habit. This is a result of the wondrous relationship between the heart and limbs, the self and the body. Every attribute that appears in the heart leaves traces on the limbs, until they do not move except in accordance with it. And every action of the limbs can leave traces in the heart, so the relationship is reciprocal.

The one who wants to become a legal scholar of deep understanding (*faqīh al-nafs*) must undertake the works of such scholars, i.e., repeated study of legal texts and keeping the company of jurists, until he is characterized by legal understanding, and becomes such a jurist. Likewise, the one who seeks to purify his self, perfect it, and adorn it with noble traits and good works has no way to achieve this except in the same manner. Just as the student of law cannot become a jurist by a night's study or reading, the one seeking to purify his self cannot achieve it by a night's worship, or be debarred from it by a day's disobedience. However, a day's neglect could lead to another until, little by little, the self becomes accustomed to negligence and leaves its striving.

Thus, good character traits may be present in some cases by innate disposition and nature. More commonly, however, they must be acquired by accustoming oneself to performing good works, observing those of good works and keeping their company. They are the worthy associates and brethren in godliness, for natures acquire both good and bad from the company one keeps. One for whom all three means[20] are present is highly noble in state, whereas one with a base disposition, who has bad companions from whom he learns, until the means to bad deeds become easy for him, is extremely far from Allāh. Between the two stations are those more or less able to acquire these means, each with a station of closeness or distance depending on their state and situation. "And whoever does an atom's weight of good will see it then, and whoever does an atom's weight of evil will see it then" (Qur'ān 99:7–8). "We wronged them not, but they wronged themselves" (Qur'ān 2:57).

Know too that at the root of good character is humility (*tawāḍuʿ*)[21] and making one's intention sincerely for Allāh. The root of base character is arrogance (*kibr*)[22] and thinking highly of oneself. Whoever is free from these has been saved from all ill. Whoever is humble for the sake of Allāh is raised by Allāh and is shielded from the diseases of the lower self, and Allāh knows best.

Whoever seeks more details on how to cure the sicknesses of the heart ought to read Imām Ghazālī's *Iḥyā'* (may Allāh have mercy on him). In this chapter, we have mentioned only the necessary minimum of ḥadīths that warn against base character and encourage good character. Whoever seeks more comprehensive treatment ought to check more detailed ḥadīth collections, such as Imām Mundhirī's *Al-Targhīb wa 'l-Tarhīb* (may Allāh have mercy on him). The basis of this entire chapter is the word of Allāh Most High, "He is indeed

---

20 The three means, as mentioned previously, are making oneself used to performing good works, observing those of good works, and keeping their company.

21 Kumushkhānawī said: "Know that humility (*tawāḍuʿ*) is among the greatest, most beautiful and most noble of praiseworthy traits. By humility the Prophet ﷺ was made superior to the first and last [of creation], for he ﷺ was the most humble of men. He was given the choice between being a king-prophet or a slave-prophet, and chose the latter. . . . From his humility was that he used to ride a donkey, let others ride with him, visit the poor, milk his own goats, raise his garments [for long garments were considered a sign of arrogance], fix his own sandals, serve himself, feed his animals, tidy his house, tie his donkey, eat with servants and workers, and carry his own provision from the market" (*Jāmiʿ al-Uṣūl fī 'l-Awliyā'* 31).

22 The Prophet ﷺ said, "One who has even a mustard-seed of arrogance (*kibr*) shall not enter the Garden" (*Muslim* and others).

successful who purifies it [the heart or lower self], and he is indeed a failure who stunts it" (Qur'ān 91:9–10).

It is indeed strange how many neither direct themselves toward eternal success nor seek it, being content instead with failure and loss. O Allāh! guide us to the best of character and works, for none guides to the best of them except You. There is no ability or power except through You, and no recourse or safety from You except in You.

## The Ḥadīths

23. Abū Hurayra ﷺ reported that the Messenger of Allāh ﷺ said,

> Beware of envy (*ḥasad*),[23] for it consumes good works as fire consumes wood (*Abū Dāwūd* and others, with good chains).

24. He also reported that the Messenger of Allāh ﷺ said,

> The strong man is not one who physically overcomes others. Nay, strong is the one who can control himself when angry (*Bukhārī* and *Muslim*).

25. Maḥmūd ibn Labīd ﷺ reported that the Messenger of Allāh ﷺ said,

> What I fear for you most is the lesser polytheism, namely, showing-off in spiritual works (*riyā'*)[24] (*Aḥmad*, with an authentic chain of transmitters).

---

23 Envy (*ḥasad*) is, "to wish that the one envied cease to have something good" (*Kashshāf Iṣṭilāḥāt al-Funūn* 1:665). Shaykh Nuh Keller comments that, "All are unlawful, and all object to Allāh's dividing His favor among His servants as He wills, which is ignorance. Allāh Most High says in Sūrat al-Zukhruf; 'Are they the ones who apportion the mercy of your Lord? It is We who have divided their livelihoods among them in this life and raised some of them in degrees above others' (Qur'ān 43: 32)" (*The Shādhilī Ṭarīqa* 54).

24 Imām Barkāwī explained that showing-off in spiritual works (*riyā'*) is "to seek a worldly benefit by a next-worldly action, or by what indicates such an actions [such as having dried lips and speaking in a low voice in order to show that one is fasting], or by telling people about it, without being forced to. Its opposite is sincerity (*ikhlāṣ*) which is to make drawing closer to Allāh one's only goal in an act of worship, without seeking a worldly benefit or to tell people. The fruit of sincerity is spiritual excellence, which is "to worship Allāh as if you see

26. Abū Hurayra ﷺ reported that the Messenger of Allāh ﷺ said,

Beware of suspicion, for suspicion is the most false of speech (*Bukhārī* and *Muslim*).

27. Abū Hurayra also reported that

a man asked, "O Messenger of Allāh, counsel me." He ﷺ replied, "Do not become angry." The man asked again repeatedly. He said, "Do not become angry" (*Bukhārī*).

28. Khawla al-Anṣārīyya ﷺ reported that the Messenger of Allāh ﷺ said,

Certain people trade in the bounty of Allāh without right, so they shall have the Fire on the Day of Resurrection" (*Bukhārī*).

29. Abū Dharr ﷺ reports from the Messenger of Allāh ﷺ who reports from his Lord, who said,

My servants, I have made injustice forbidden to Myself, and I have made it forbidden to you, so do not be unjust (*Muslim*).

30. It is reported by Abū Hurayra ﷺ that

the Messenger of Allāh ﷺ asked, "Do you know what backbiting (*ghība*) is?" They replied, "Allāh and His Messenger know best." He said, "Mentioning your brother by what he dislikes." It was asked, "What if my brother is as I say?" He said, "If he is as you say, you have backbit him, and if he is not, you have slandered him" (*Muslim*).

31. It is reported by Abū Hurayra ﷺ that the Messenger of Allāh ﷺ said:

Do not envy each other. Do not raise prices against each other. Do not hate each other. Do not turn away from each other. And do not undercut each other. Rather, be, O servants of Allāh, brothers. A

---

Him, for though you see Him not, know that He sees you'" (*Al-Barīqa al-Maḥmūdiyya fī Sharḥ al-Ṭarīqa al-Muḥammadīyya* 2:84–85).

> Muslim is a Muslim's brother. He neither wrongs him, nor cheats him, nor does he tell him lies, nor does he have contempt for him. Piety (*taqwā*) is here," and he pointed to his chest. "It is sufficient evil for a man to look down upon his Muslim brother. All of a Muslim is inviolable to another Muslim: his blood, his wealth, and his honor" (*Bukhārī* and *Muslim*, with the latter's wording).

32. It is reported by Ibn ʿAbbās ﷺ that the Messenger of Allāh ﷺ said,

> Do not quarrel with your brother, nor jest with him.[25] And do not make an appointment with him and then break it (*Tirmidhī*).

33. It is reported by Abū 'l-Dardā' ﷺ that the Messenger of Allāh ﷺ said,

> Allāh hates the obscene and wasteful (*Tirmidhī*; it is rigorously authenticated).

34. It is reported by Ibn Masʿūd ﷺ that the Messenger of Allāh ﷺ said,

> The believer does not insult, nor curse, nor is he obscene or wasteful (*Tirmidhī* and Bukhārī in *al-Ādāb al-Mufrad*).

35. It is reported by ʿĀ'isha ﷺ that the Messenger of Allāh ﷺ said,

> Do not insult the dead, for they have moved on to what they sent forth (*Bukhārī; Abū Dāwūd* has: "If your companion dies, pray for him and do not talk ill of him").

36. It is reported by Ḥudhayfa ﷺ that the Messenger of Allāh ﷺ said,

> The busy talebearer shall not enter the Garden (*Bukhārī* and *Muslim*).

---

25 Imām Munāwī explains that "nor jest with him" means in a way that he dislikes. The scholars explain that prohibited jesting is that which is excessive, constant, or harmful (*Fayḍ al-Qadīr* 6:421).

37. It is reported by Anas ﷺ that the Messenger of Allāh ﷺ said,

> Whoever withholds his anger, Allāh withholds his punishment from him (Ṭabarānī in *al-Awsaṭ*, and it has a supporting narration from Ibn ʿUmar ﷺ related by Ibn Abī 'l-Dunyā).

38. It is reported by Ibn ʿAbbās ﷺ that the Messenger of Allāh ﷺ said,

> Whoever eavesdrops on the conversation of people who dislike to have him listening shall have molten lead poured into his ears on the Day of Judgment (*Bukhārī*).

39. It is reported by Abū Saʿīd al-Khudrī ﷺ that the Messenger of Allāh ﷺ said,

> Two traits are not found together in a believer: stinginess and bad character (*Tirmidhī*).

40. The previous ḥadīth is supported by Abū Hurayra's report, as narrated by Bukhārī in *al-Adāb*, that the Messenger of Allāh ﷺ said,

> Stinginess (*shuḥḥ*) and faith are never found together with bad character in a servant's heart.

41. It is reported by Anas ﷺ that the Messenger of Allāh ﷺ said,

> Glad tidings to the one busied by his own faults from the faults of others (*Bazzār*, with a good chain).

42. The previous ḥadīth is supported by Abdullāh ibn ʿAbbās's report, as narrated by Bukhārī in *al-Adab* (*al-Mufrad*), that the Messenger of Allāh ﷺ said,

> If you are eager to know your companion's faults, then look first at your own faults.

43. It is reported by Ibn ʿUmar ﷺ that the Messenger of Allāh ﷺ said,

Whoever thinks highly of himself and struts in his walk shall meet Allāh while He is angry (*Ḥākim;* its transmitters are trustworthy).

44. It is reported by Ibn Masʿūd ﷺ with the words:

One who has even a mustard seed's weight of arrogance (*kibr*) shall not enter the Garden (*Muslim* and others).

45. It is reported by Sahl ibn Saʿd ﷺ that the Messenger of Allāh ﷺ said,

Haste is from Satan (*Tirmidhī;* it is well authenticated).

46. Muṣʿab ibn Saʿd reported this from his father with the words:

Deliberation is good in all things except in matters of the Next Life (*Abū Dāwūd,* and *Ḥākim;* it is rigorously authenticated).

47. It is reported by Muʿādh ibn Jabal ﷺ that the Messenger of Allāh ﷺ said,

Whoever scolds his brother for a sin [he did in the past] shall not die until he does it (*Tirmidhī;* it is well authenticated).

48. It is reported by Bahz ibn Ḥakīm from his father from his grandfather ﷺ that the Messenger of Allāh ﷺ said,

Woe to the one who lies to make people laugh, woe to him, woe to him (*Abū Dāwūd, Tirmidhī* and *Nasāʾī,* with a strong chain).

49. It is reported by Anas ﷺ that the Messenger of Allāh ﷺ said,

The expiation due to one you have slandered is to seek forgiveness for him (Ḥārith ibn Abī Usāma, with a weak chain).

50. It is reported from ʿĀʾisha ﷺ that the Messenger of Allāh ﷺ said,

The most hated of people to Allāh is one who constantly argues (*Bukhārī* and *Muslim*).

# Encouraging Good Character

51. It is reported by Ibn Masʿūd ﷺ that the Messenger of Allāh ﷺ said,

> Be truthful, for truthfulness leads to righteousness and righteousness leads to the Garden. A man continues to be truthful and stands by the truth until he is written as truthful with Allāh. And beware of lying, for lying leads to obscenity, and obscenity leads to the Fire. A man continues to lie and adheres to lying until he is written as a liar with Allāh (*Bukhārī* and *Muslim*).

52. It is reported by Muʿāwiya ﷺ that the Messenger of Allāh ﷺ said,

> Whoever Allāh desires good for, He gives him profound understanding (*fiqh*) of religion (*Bukhārī* and *Muslim*).

53. It is reported by Abū 'l-Dardā' ﷺ that the Messenger of Allāh ﷺ said,

> Nothing weighs heavier upon the Scales than good character[26] (*Abū Dāwūd*, and *Tirmidhī*; it is rigorously authenticated).

26 Said Shaykh al-Islām Muṣṭafā al-ʿArūsī in his super-commentary on Zakarīyyā

54. It is reported by Abū Hurayra ﷺ that the Messenger of Allāh ﷺ said,

Piety and good character are what enter most people into the Garden. (*Tirmidhī*; Ḥākim deemed it is rigorously authenticated).

55. It is also reported by Abū Hurayra ﷺ that the Messenger of Allāh ﷺ said,

You cannot reach all people with your wealth, so let your smiling face and good character reach them (Abū Yaʿlā; Ḥākim deemed it rigorously authenticated).

56. It is reported by Ibn ʿUmar ﷺ that the Messenger of Allāh ﷺ said,

Shyness (*ḥayā'*) is from faith (*Bukhārī* and *Muslim*).

57. It is reported by Ibn Masʿūd ﷺ that the Messenger of Allāh ﷺ said,

Among the words of the previous prophets that have reached people are, "If you feel no shyness, then do as you wish"[27] (*Bukhārī* and *Abū Dāwūd*).

58. It is reported by Abū Hurayra ﷺ that the Messenger of Allāh ﷺ said,

The strong believer is better and more beloved to Allāh than the weak believer, though there is good in both. Be avid for what benefits you. Rely upon Allāh, and do not be weak. If anything befalls

---

al-Anṣārī's commentary on Imām Qushayrī's *Risāla*, "Know that good character is among the greatest blessings that Allāh bestowed upon his most beloved slaves who were granted proximity, for its fruits are manifest both in this life and in the Hereafter" (*Natā'ij al-Afkār al-Qudsiyya fī Bayān Maʿānī Sharḥ al-Risāla al-Qushayriyya* 3:185).

27 Munāwī said: "If you feel no shame, then do as you wish," you will be reckoned for it, so it is a stern warning for the one who is shameless (*Fayḍ al-Qadīr*, 2: 540).

you, do not say, "If only I had done such and such," rather, say, "Allāh decreed, and what He willed happened," for "if only" opens the door for Satan (*Muslim*).

59. It is reported by ʿIyād ibn Ḥimār ﷺ that the Messenger of Allāh ﷺ said,

> Allāh has revealed to me that you should be humble, so that none transgresses against another, and none boasts before another (*Muslim*).

60. It is reported by Abū 'l-Dardā' ﷺ that the Messenger of Allāh ﷺ said,

> Whoever protects the honor of his brother in his absence, Allāh protects his face from the fire on the Day of Resurrection (*Tirmidhī*; it is well authenticated).

61. It is reported by ʿAbdullāh ibn Salām ﷺ that the Messenger of Allāh ﷺ said,

> O people, spread *salāms*, mend family relations, feed others, and pray while others sleep, and you shall enter the Garden safely (*Tirmidhī*; it is rigorously authenticated).

62. It is reported by Abū Hurayra ﷺ that the Messenger of Allāh ﷺ said,

> A believer is the mirror of his believing brother (*Abū Dāwūd*, with an authentic chain).

63. It is reported by Ibn ʿUmar ﷺ that the Messenger of Allāh ﷺ said,

> A believer who mixes with people and bears their harm is better than one who does not mix with people and does not bear their harm. (*Ibn Māja*, with an authentic chain; and *Tirmidhī*, without mention of the Companion who narrated it).

# Remembrance & Supplication

The weak servant [Imām Ẓafar ʿUthmānī (may Allāh have mercy on him)] says:

Those who have seen with the light of spiritual insight (*baṣīra*) realize that there is no salvation except in meeting Allāh Most High, and that there is no means to this meeting except through the servant dying as a lover and knower of Allāh. They have understood that love and intimacy are not possible except by constant remembrance of the Beloved, and by remaining steadfast in it. Likewise, knowledge of Allāh is not possible except by constant contemplation (*fikr*) of His attributes and actions, for there is nothing in existence except Allāh Most High and His actions.[28] They have also realized that constant remembrance and contemplation is not possible except by bidding farewell to the world[29] and its temptations, and to seek from it only to the extent of one's necessity and need. This is not possible except

28 This means that nothing has absolute independent existence except Allāh Most High. Everything besides Allāh is from His actions.

29 Ibn ʿAṭāʾillāh explained the "world" and "worldly" in their blameworthy sense in his aphorism "The worldly is that which distracts you from Allāh."

by filling one's time, night and day, with remembrance and contemplation. Thus, whoever seeks to enter the Garden without account (*ḥisāb*) should fill his time with acts of obedience.[30] And whoever wishes that good works weigh heavily on his scale, let him occupy his time with acts of obedience.

Allāh Most High told the closest and highest in rank of his servants ﷺ, "Lo! By day you have a chain of business. So remember the name of your Lord and give yourself with complete devotion" (Qur'ān 73:8). He said, "Remember the name of your Lord morning and evening. And worship Him [a portion] of the night. And glorify Him through the livelong night" (Qur'ān 76:25). And He said, "Lo! The vigil of the night is (a time) when impression is more keen and speech more certain" (Qur'ān 73:6). The verses and ḥadīths about the merits of remembrance and supplication are many, and His words, "Therefore, remember Me, and I will remember you," (Qur'ān 2:152) are sufficient glad tidings to one whose Lord remembers him. Or His saying, "Call upon me, and I will answer you" (Qur'ān 40:60). Glad tidings indeed to one whose call Allāh answers. Had there been no other merit in remembrance it would have sufficed. What, then, if it is the proclamation of electhood (*wilāya*),[31] the means to closeness, salvation, and ennoblement?

At the same time, remembrance of Allāh is the strongest means to acts of obedience and good character, and the firmest deterrent against sins, bad deeds, and base character. For remembrance of Allāh is light, and what light! By it hearts find rest, breasts are expanded, and continue to expand by acts of obedience, just as this light contracts and constricts by sins and bad deeds. Such missteps are harder on the one

---

30 Merely permissible actions can become acts of worship that one is rewarded for through high noble intentions.

31 Imām Qushayrī quoted his teacher Abū ʿAlī al-Daqqāq, who said, "Remembrance of Allāh is the proclamation of electhood (*wilāya*). So whoever has been granted remembrance of Allāh has been granted the proclamation." Shaykh al-Islām Zakariyyā al-Anṣārī explained that, "It is the means to draw closer and reach Allāh, so it bears witness to electhood. And Allāh Most High said, 'Call upon me, I will answer you,' with My protection and honoring" (*Sharḥ al-Risāla al-Qushayriyya* 3:157).

who makes much remembrance (*dhākir*) than falling off a mountain, and heavier to his heart than losing wealth, family, or strength. This forces him to repent and turn penitently to his Lord, so that his light returns to its previous state, and he does not dare to return to a like action in the future.

We have mentioned the necessary minimum in this chapter of ḥadīths on the merits of remembrance and supplication, without encompassing the topic.

It is clear to any Muslim that the best of remembrance is reciting the Qur'ān, for it is radiance and light. By it, there is salvation from delusions, and a healing for hearts. Whoever amongst the tyrannical opposes the Qur'ān is destroyed by Allāh, and whoever seeks knowledge in other than it, Allāh leads him astray. The Qur'ān is the secure rope of Allāh, His manifest light, and firm handhold. It is the most dependable of things to rely upon, whose wonders are unceasing and marvels unending. Scholars can place no limit on its beneficial knowledge. Reciters find no weariness in its constant repetition. It is what guided the first and the last. When the *jinn* heard it, they immediately returned to their people as heralds and said, "Lo! We have heard a marvelous Qur'ān, which guides unto righteousness, so we believe in it and ascribe none unto our Lord" (Qur'ān 72:1–2). Whoever believes in it has been given success (*tawfiq*), whoever preaches it has spoken the trust; whoever holds fast to it has been guided; and whoever acts upon it has triumphed.

Allāh Most High has said, "We reveal the Reminder, and lo! We are its Guardian" (Qur'ān 15:9). Among the means of preserving it in hearts and writing is persistence in its recitation and study, for the Prophet ﷺ said, "The best of you are those who learn the Qur'ān and teach it," as related by Bukhārī. Tirmidhī relates from Abū Saʿīd ؓ, "Whoever is busied by the Qur'ān from remembering or asking me, I shall give him the best of what I give those who ask." Nasā'ī in his *Kubrā*, Ibn Māja, and Ḥākim relate with an authentic chain from Anas ؓ that the Messenger of Allāh ﷺ said, "The people of the Qur'ān are the people of Allāh and His elect." The ḥadīths on the virtues of the

Qur'ān and its recital are numerous and well known. Most of them are recorded in the authentic collections.

The scholars are in unanimous agreement (*ijmā*ʿ) that there is no worship of the tongue after reciting the Qur'ān as virtuous as the remembrance of Allāh and raising one's needs to Allāh Most High through supplication. It is clear that following the reported supplications (*ma'thūr*) of the Prophet ﷺ and his Companions is superior and more meritorious, even if it is permitted to make remembrance of Allāh in any language and in any manner, as is evident.

This quashes the arguments of those who say that the Sufis have themselves made up invocations without a basis in the Prophetic Sunna, such as the remembrance of affirmation by saying *illa 'Llāh* [but Allāh],[32] or remembrance with the name of the Essence, *Allāh Allāh*. The answer is that this has the same basis as translating the Qur'ān into a foreign language, or mentioning Allāh with the corresponding name in it. It is not lost on anyone that saying *Ē Khudā, Ē Kardagār* [O Lord, O Doer] is remembrance of Allāh, even if not transmitted from the Prophet ﷺ.

The Sufis used these invocations because remembrance (*dhikr*) for them is the opposite of forgetfulness (*nisyān*) and every remembrance accompanied by heedlessness (*ghafla*) and forgetfulness is not remembrance of [true] value in their eyes. They also saw that remembrance through brief statements often becomes firm in the heart more quickly than remembrance through complete phrases. Therefore, they sometimes taught the invocation of the name of the Essence. Sometimes invoking with *illa 'Llāh, illa 'Llāh* (but Allāh, but Allāh) until remembrance becomes firmly established in the heart such that when the tongue utters the remembrance of Allāh, the heart utters with it and is not absent. After this they placed primary emphasis on the invocations transmitted from the Prophet ﷺ such as *Lā ilāha illa 'Llāh* (there is no god but Allāh), *Subḥān Allāh* (glory

32 This is abbreviated from the statement of oneness, *lā ilāha illa 'Llāh* (there is no god but Allāh).

be to Allāh), *Al-ḥamdu li 'Llāh* (all praise is for Allāh), *Allāhu akbar* (Allāh is greatest), *Lā ḥawla wa lā qūwwata illa bi 'Llāh* (there is no ability nor power except by Allāh).

The invocations that the Sufi spiritual guides compiled, even though they are not transmitted from the Prophet ﷺ, act as initial means for the heart to accept and prepare for these transmitted invocations.[33] This is similar to reciting the Qur'ān syllable by syllable when teaching children, which is not actual recitation of the Qur'ān because of the breakdown. Even the one in a state of major ritual impurity, or a menstruating woman can recite in this manner. However, it is clearly an initial means to proper recitation, for this is how a child learns to recite, and there is no other means to it but this. Likewise, those still children on the spiritual path have no way to make the remembrance of Allāh firm in their hearts except in the aforementioned manner.

Know, then, that the goal of Sufism is to achieve proximity and Allāh's good pleasure in the Hereafter, and achieving the rejoicing of faith (*bashāshat al-īmān*) and its unfolding in the heart in this life. This to them is knowledge of Allāh, and it is a great bounty. This rejoicing of faith is mentioned in the ḥadīth of Ibn ʿAbbās ؓ regarding the story of Heraclius, as reported by Bukhārī. Ibn ʿAbbās ؓ said, "Likewise the rejoicing of faith when it mixes with the rejoicing of hearts (*bashāshat al-qulūb*)."

---

33 The Muftī of Beirut Shaykh Muṣṭafā Najā, explains that "The litanies (*awrād*) were placed for intimate discourse (*munājāt*) with and manifesting one's humility in the presence of Allāh, while fulfilling the duties of slavehood to Him Most High. The scholars say that these litanies did not generally exist in the beginning of Islām, nor in the very first age. However, they were collected by the people of Allāh to arouse the desire of seekers towards the Sought, Allāh Most High, and in order to open the door to Him so that even common believers could enter, for they saw a general weakness of spiritual will and determination, with heedlessness taking over hearts and certainty waning. It is incumbent upon anyone who commits himself to performing a litany, of remembrance, prayer, or other spiritual works, to be consistent in it and not to leave it without excuse, especially if one made a covenant with one's spiritual guide to perform it. Then, if one misses a night litany, one makes it up in the day and vice versa" (*Kitāb Kashf al-Asrār li Tanwīr al-Afkār* 60).

This noble ascription is almost never realized except through the company of the perfected spiritual guides whose hearts have been illumined by the light of this tremendous ascription, which continues to be passed down from heart to heart, and whose source is the niche of prophethood and the basin of messengerhood, the heart of our Noble Master Muḥammad ﷺ.

As for spiritual struggles, performing good works, and acquiring good character, these may be possible without the company of a spiritual guide. However, acquiring these in their company with a keen spiritual will (*himma*) is realized with relative ease, and, outside their company, with much difficulty and hardship.

The outward semblance of the Sufis, such as listening to spiritual poetry (*samāʿ*), celebrations, gatherings, and the like, are not of central importance, however. Shaykh Shāh Walī Allāh [al-Dehlawī] (may Allāh sanctify his secret) said, "The spiritual ascription of the Sufis is a great bounty. As for their outward semblance, it is of little weight." That is why it is seen that the realized Sufis do not limit themselves to the outward semblance. Rather, their only goal is to call people to the remembrance of Allāh and His obedience, to acquiring the character traits of Allāh's Beloved Prophet Muḥammad ﷺ and following his example. Such men desire to direct people away from being deluded by this world, to incline towards the next life, to warn them of the enticing of the lower self (*al-nafs al-ammāra*) and the deceptions of Iblīs the Accursed.

The sign of these realized Sufis is mentioned in the ḥadīth: "If they are seen, Allāh is remembered," and in the Qur'ān, "The mark of them is on their foreheads from the traces of prostration" (48:29). Among their signs is that the fire of the love of the world is extinguished in the heart when one attends their gatherings, and the heart directs itself to Allāh, and seeks His good pleasure when it hears their words. As for other signs, such as miracles, preternatural occurrences, and answered supplications, these are not necessary for electhood (*wilāya*), and are only bestowed by the pure generosity and benevolence of Allāh.

## The Ḥadīths

64. It is reported by Abū Hurayra ؓ that the Messenger of Allāh ﷺ said,

> Allāh Most High says, "I am with my servant when he remembers Me and his lips move with My remembrance." (*Ibn Māja;* Ibn Ḥibbān declared it to be rigorously authentic; Bukhārī quoted it without mention of its chain).

65. It is reported by Muʿādh ibn Jabal ؓ that the Messenger of Allāh ﷺ said,

> The son of Adam does no work closer to warding off Allāh's punishment than the remembrance of Allāh (*Ibn Abī Shayba* and *Ṭabarānī,* with an authentic chain).

66. It is reported by Abū Hurayra ؓ that the Messenger of Allāh ﷺ said,

> No people gather together to make remembrance of Allāh but that the angels encircle them, Mercy envelops them, and Allāh remembers them with those nigh unto Him (*Muslim*).

67. It is also reported by Abū Hurayra (may Allāh be pleased with him) that the Messenger of Allāh ﷺ said,

> No people sit without remembrance of Allāh and without sending blessings upon the Prophet ﷺ except that it is a woe upon them on the Day of Resurrection (*Tirmidhī;* it is authentic).

68. It is reported by Nuʿmān ibn Bashīr ؓ that the Messenger of Allāh ﷺ said,

> Supplication is worship (*Abū Dāwūd, Tirmidhī, Nasā'ī* and *Ibn Māja;* Tirmidhī deemed it rigorously authenticated).

69. Tirmidhī also relates from Anas ؓ that the Messenger of Allāh ﷺ said,

Supplication is the essence of worship.

70. Tirmidhī also relates from Abū Hurayra ﷺ that the Messenger of Allāh ﷺ said,

Nothing is more dear to Allāh than supplication.

71. It is reported by Salmān ﷺ that the Messenger of Allāh ﷺ said,

Verily your Lord is reluctant and generous. He is reluctant to leave His servant's hands empty when he raises them (in supplication) (*Abū Dāwūd, Tirmidhī,* and *Ibn Māja*).

72. It is reported by Anas ﷺ that the Messenger of Allāh ﷺ said,

Supplication between the *adhān* and *iqāma* is not rejected (*Nasā'ī* and others; Ibn Ḥibbān said it is rigorously authenticated).

73. It is reported by Ibn Masʿūd ﷺ that the Messenger of Allāh ﷺ said,

The people most deserving of me on the Day of Resurrection are those most constant in sending blessings upon me (*Tirmidhī* and *Ibn Ḥibbān;* it is rigorously authenticated).

74. It is reported by Shaddād ibn Aws ﷺ that the Messenger of Allāh ﷺ said,

The best supplication of forgiveness (*sayyid al-istighfār*) is to say, "O Allāh, You are my Lord. There is no god but You. You created me and I am Your slave. I follow Your covenant and promise as much as I am able. I seek refuge in you from the evil of what I have done. I recognize my sin, so forgive me, for only You can forgive sins" (*Bukhārī*).

75. Tirmidhī and Abū Dāwūd relate with a sound chain from Bilāl ibn Yasār ibn Zayd, from his father, from his grandfather, that he heard the Prophet ﷺ say,

Whoever says, "I seek the forgiveness of Allāh, there is no god but

Him, the Living the Self-Subsistent, and I repent to him," is forgiven, even if he has fled from the front-lines.

76. It is reported by Abū Saʿīd al-Khudrī ﷺ that the Messenger of Allāh ﷺ said,

> The lasting acts of righteousness are: "There is no god but Allāh, Allāh is exalted beyond all limits, Allāh is the greatest, praise be to Allāh, and there is no ability nor power except by Allāh" (*Nasā'ī*, and both Ibn Ḥibbān and Ḥākim said it is rigorously authenticated).

77. It is reported by Samura ibn Jundub ﷺ that the Messenger of Allāh ﷺ said,

> The most beloved of words to Allāh are four, and it does not matter which one you begin with: Glory be to Allāh, all praise is for Allāh, there is no god but Allāh, and Allāh is the greatest (*Muslim*).

78. It is reported by Ibn ʿUmar ﷺ that

> the Messenger of Allāh ﷺ would not leave the following words each evening and morning, "O Allāh, I ask you for pardon and well-being in my religion, worldly affairs, family and wealth. O Allāh, cover my faults, and calm my fears. Protect me from the front, back, right, left, and above, and I seek refuge from being harmed from below" (*Nasā'ī* and *Ibn Māja*: Ḥākim deemed it rigorously authenticated).

79. It is reported by Ibn ʿUmar ﷺ that the Messenger of Allāh ﷺ used to say,

> O Allāh, I seek refuge in you from the cessation of your blessings, the reversal of the well-being You granted, the suddenness of your vengeance, and from Your displeasure (*Muslim*).

80. It is reported by Abū Hurayra ﷺ that the Messenger of Allāh ﷺ used to say,

> O Allāh, make good my religion that is my safeguard, and make good

the worldly life that I live, and make good my next life to which I go forth. Make my life an increase in all good, and my death a rest from all evil (*Muslim*).

81. It is reported by Anas ﷺ that Prophet ﷺ said,

> Our Lord! Give unto us in the world that which is good and in the Hereafter that which is good, and guard us from the doom of Fire (*Bukhārī* and *Muslim*).

82. It is reported by Anas ﷺ that the Messenger of Allāh ﷺ used to say,

> O Allāh, aid me through what you have taught me, teach me that which profits me, and give me beneficial knowledge (*Nasā'ī* and *Ḥākim*).

83. It is reported by ʿĀ'isha ﷺ that the Prophet ﷺ taught them the following supplication,

> O Allāh, I ask you for all good, present and future, what I know of and what I know not. And I seek refuge in you from all evil, present and future, what I know of, and what I know not. O Allāh, I ask of you the best of what your Servant and Messenger ﷺ asked for, and I seek refuge from the worst of what your servant and messenger sought refuge from. O Allāh, I ask You to grant me the Garden, and that which leads to it of words and actions. I seek refuge in You from the fire and that which leads to it of words and actions. And I ask that You make all that You have decreed for me to be good (*Ibn Māja, Ḥākim,* and *Ibn Ḥibbān;* the latter two deemed it rigorously authenticated).

84. It is reported by Abū Hurayra ﷺ that the Messenger of Allāh ﷺ said,

> Two phrases beloved to the Merciful, light on the tongue and heavy on the Scale, are *Subḥāna 'Llāhi wa bi ḥamdihī Subḥāna 'Llāhi 'l-ʿAẓīm*

["Glory be to Allāh and all praise, glory be to Allāh the Great"] (*Bukhārī* and *Muslim*).

Imām Ẓafar ʿUthmānī comments:

This is the last ḥadīth recorded by Imām Bukhārī (may Allāh have mercy on him) in his *Ṣaḥīḥ*, and he was followed in this by several ḥadīth masters in their collections. This ḥadīth shows the immense vastness of the mercy of Allāh, for He gives tremendous rewards for small actions. So glory be to Allāh and all praise, glory be to Allāh the Great. Glory be to You, O Allāh, and all praise. I bear witness that there is no god but You, I seek Your forgiveness and repent unto you. O Allāh, there is no blessing that reaches me or any of Your creation in the day, or in the night, except that it is from You, the One who has no partner. So all praise and thanks are due to You, thanks that have no end but Your good pleasure. O Allāh, bless, bestow peace and bounties upon the Master of Your prophets and messengers, the best of Your creation and the Chosen One, our Master Muḥammad, and his Family and Companions, to the extent of Your blessings and gifts. And our last words are that all praise belongs to Allāh, the Lord of the worlds.

# Biographies of the Commentators

### Imām Kumushkhānawī

Aḥmad Ḍiyā' al-Dīn ibn Muṣṭafā al-Kumushkhānawī was born in Kumushkhāna, 1227 AH. In his youth he traveled to Āstāna to seek knowledge from the top scholars of Ottoman Turkey. His spiritual guide and teacher in ḥadīth was the noble master Shaykh Aḥmad ibn Sulaymān al-Arwādī.

Mawlānā Kumushkhānawī was a spiritual guide of the Khālidī Naqshabandī path, and a distinguished scholar of ḥadīth. He compiled *Rāmūz al-Ḥadīth*, a large collection of ḥadīths arranged alphabetically, along the lines of Imām al-Suyūṭī's *al-Jāmiᶜ al-Ṣaghīr*. He also authored a five volume commentary on it called *Lawāmiᶜ al-ᶜUqūl*. He taught *Rāmūz al-Ḥadīth* about seventy times in his Sufi lodge (*khānaqāh*). He used to gift students of knowledge this book but took a small monetary deposit, which would be returned upon attending a complete reading of the text. This practice was also followed by his students across Turkey, as a result of which the book's fame spread across the heart of the Islāmic Caliphate, and virtually every scholar and student possessed a copy. One of his principal goals in this practice was to revive knowledge and implementation of the prophetic example.

He founded a successful religious endowment in which he and the affluent of his followers placed a large sum of money to be borrowed by those in need, as a substitute for the usurious banking system that had begun creeping in.

He authored over fifty books, mainly in Sufism and ḥadīth, and was considered by Imām Muḥammad Zāhid al-Kawtharī to have been the reviver (*mujaddid*) at the turn of the 14th Islāmic Century, for "he revived the Prophetic example and sciences after they had waned in the Ottoman lands . . . and thousands of accomplished gnostics were guided by his spiritual instruction."

After a life of teaching and spiritual guidance, he passed away in 1311 AH, and was buried in the graveyard of Sulṭān Sulaymān in Istanbul (*Al-Taḥrīr al-Wajīz* 47–51, and *Irghām al-Marīd* 69–76).

## Mullā ʿAlī al-Qārī

Imām Mullā Nūr al-Dīn ʿAlī ibn Sulṭān Muḥammad was the top Ḥanafī scholar and ḥadīth master of his time. Imām Lakhnawī and others held that he may well have been the reviver (*mujaddid*) at the turn of the 11th Islāmic Century. He earned his name al-Qārī, "The Reciter," because of his mastery of the sciences of Qur'ānic recitation.

After migrating from his birthplace, Herat, Afghanistan, he lived the rest of his life in Makka, where he studied with the top scholars of his age, including Abū 'l-Ḥasan al-Bakrī, Ibn Ḥajar al-Haytamī, ʿAbdullāh al-Sindī, and Quṭb al-Dīn al-Makkī.

He authored a large number of works in Ḥanafī jurisprudence, fundamentals of Islāmic faith, the sciences of ḥadīth, Sufism, history, Arabic lexicography, and Qur'ānic exegesis. His most famous works are his outstanding, detailed commentary on Tabrīzī's ḥadīth collection, *Mishkāt al-Maṣābīḥ*, called *Mirqāt al-Mafātīḥ Sharḥ Mishkāt al-Maṣābīḥ*; a commentary on Qāḍī ʿIyāḍ's book on the Prophet ﷺ,

*Al-Shifā'*; and a commentary on Imām Tirmidhī's *Shamā'il*. His most famous work in jurisprudence is his *Fatḥ Bāb al-ʿInāya*, a three-volume commentary distinguished by its clear explanation and decisive presentation of the key evidences from the Qur'ān and ḥadīth for the rulings of the Ḥanafī school of sacred law.

But the most frequently used of his works is his litany of Prophetic supplications, *Al-Ḥizb al-Aʿẓam* (The supreme daily *dhikr*), in which he gathered hundreds of prophetic supplications and divided them in seven parts, one to be read each day of the week.

He lived a life of piety and godfearingness, in which he stayed far from any official positions and earned his income by writing out one or two copies of the Holy Qur'ān each year, embellished with marginal commentary, for he was also one of the greatest calligraphers of his time. He died in Makka in 1014/1606 (*Al-Fawā'id al-Bahiyya* 25; *Al-Imām ʿAlī al-Qārī wa Āthāruhū fī ʿIlm al-Ḥadīth*, *Reliance of the Traveler* 1038–9).

# About the Translator

Faraz Rabbani is a researcher and teacher of the Islamic sciences, specializing in Islamic Law. He is a teacher with the Razi Institute, a Toronto-based educational project; the Director of SeekersMedia (www.SeekersMedia.com), an online Islamic media portal; and a columnist for Islamica Magazine. He obtained a Bachelor's in Economics & Commerce from the University of Toronto in 1997. After that, he studied and taught the Islamic sciences in Damascus, Amman, and Karachi for ten years, under leading Islamic scholars, including Shaykh Adīb Kallās, Shaykh Ḥassān al-Hindī, Shaykh Muḥammad Jumuʿa, Shaykh Akram ʿAbd al-Wahhāb, Shaykh Nuh Keller, and Muftī Mahmud Ashraf Usmani.

*Also from*
WHITE THREAD PRESS

*Prayers for Forgiveness*
*The Path to Perfection*
*Saviours of Islamic Spirit*
*Absolute Essentials of Islam*
*The Differences of the Imāms*
*Provisions for the Seekers*
*Ghazālī's The Beginning of Guidance*
*Reflections of Pearls*
*Fiqh al-Imam: Key Proofs in Hanafi Fiqh*
*The Islamic Laws of Animal Slaughter*
*Birth Control and Abortion in Islam*
*Ṣalāt & Salām: A Manual of Blessings on Allāh's Beloved*
*Imām Abū Ḥanīfa's Al-Fiqh al-Akbar Explained*
*Ascent to Felicity (Marāqī 'l-Saʿādāt)*
*The Book of Wisdoms (Ikmāl al-Shiyam)*
*The Shāfiʿī Manual of Purity, Prayer & Fasting*
*Al-Ḥizb al-Aʿẓam (The Supreme Daily Remembrance)*
*Handbook of a Healthy Muslim Marriage*

White Thread
PRESS

www.whitethreadpress.com